SIS,
YOU CAN
NEGOTIATE!

10 TIPS TO NEGOTIATE
YOUR SALARY OR RAISE

AIGNÉ GOLDSBY, ESQ.

authorHOUSE

AuthorHouse™
1663 Liberty Drive
Bloomington, IN 47403
www.authorhouse.com
Phone: 833-262-8899

Published by AuthorHouse   07/31/2023

ISBN: 979-8-8230-1266-9 (sc)
ISBN: 979-8-8230-1265-2 (hc)
ISBN: 979-8-8230-1264-5 (e)

Library of Congress Control Number: 2023914274

Print information available on the last page.

This book is printed on acid-free paper.

I'd like to thank God for providing me with the vision for this book. And a special thanks to Gabriella Martin for her work on designing the cover and my editor, Claudia Cramer of CSC Professional Editing and Creative Writing Services.

CONTENTS

INTRODUCTION

Have you ever been passed up for a raise or promotion? Or maybe you've recently found out one of your colleagues is making more money than you? Yea, that was me too.

Let me tell you a brief story. In August of 2016, I just graduated from law school and had taken the bar exam. I was so excited to get my first job and be a "real lawyer." But that excitement quickly turned to desperation when rent was due and my bank account was negative! I frantically applied for jobs and finally got an offer at a small law firm. "Yes! This was finally it!" My excitement for my career returned! That is until I saw my salary. I thought, *This can't be it...*, but it was.

Even though I wanted more, I was so desperate for a job, I took the offer.

Fast forward a year or so (after I was no longer employed at that law firm), I was talking to one of my former white male colleagues (one with comparable experience as me) and I found out he was making more money than I was! I was shocked, confused and upset. *I can't believe this! I worked just as hard as he did. Why was he getting paid more for the same job?* It was at that moment, I realized I had no one to blame but myself. Truth was, I knew several lawyers in my current position that were making more money than me, but weren't more qualified than I was. I ended up figuring out the reason why they were making more money than I was. It was simply because they asked. And the truth was if I knew my value, if I knew what I brought to the table, then perhaps I could have negotiated a higher salary, but I didn't. I took what was offered to me. I didn't properly advocate for my value or worth at that time.

With the legal profession dominated by white male lawyers, it can be difficult for a person of color or a woman to navigate the space. As a Black woman, especially, I can tell you, it *is* difficult. Only 5% of lawyers in the U.S. are Black and less than 2% are Black women. It's not fair. And that's why I have made it my mission to increase diversity in the legal profession and to help women who are seeking upward mobility in their careers to achieve positions that equitably affirm and compensate them based on the value they bring to the table.

Most of you reading this have probably heard the statistic that women make 83 cents for every dollar a man makes, but did you know that the statistics are even lower for women of color? Black women make 63 cents for every dollar, and Hispanic women make 54 cents for every dollar.[1] This is a perpetual cycle that is not fair and needs to be broken.

Our concepts of value and worth intentionally or unintentionally, are usually groomed during our formative years. I grew up in Pennsylvania and went to Bryn Mawr College for my Bachelors degree. I had a quick detour in New York City where I worked as

---

[1] U.S. Census Bureau, "Income and Poverty in the United States: 2020"

a Legal Assistant, then I traveled to Connecticut for graduate school, graduating from the University of Connecticut School of Law. Of course, I went on to become a lawyer and later became the Founder of Black Esquire®, a business dedicated to increasing diversity in the legal profession by raising the 5% of Black U.S. lawyers.

When it came to the negotiation of my salary, well, there was none. If I wanted to work at a firm and was offered the role I desired, I would simply accept what they offered. I mean, what they presented must be all they had *to* offer, right? I had to learn my lesson the hard way.

It's crazy to me, especially when we're talking about women, and even more specifically women of color, we don't negotiate; we don't talk about ourselves in a way where we fully acknowledge our value so that people know our worth. It is one of my life missions to help you identify your worth and get paid based on that value.

As The VALUE Coach, I am not only going to delve into 10 tips for negotiating your salary or raise, but I will add some bonus material, walking you through mock negotiations. I will also include some affirmations you can say out loud to get your mind ready and prepared to get your value. You deserve it! But first, you may ask:

What is a VALUE Coach?

As The VALUE Coach, I specifically work with Black lady leaders as I like to call them. Black women who are called to do great things like becoming a lawyer or maybe even running for a political office (two areas of which I have a great wealth of knowledge). Overall, I want to help all women assert their value with clarity and confidence so they can elevate their lives and careers. Specifically, I help them understand their value and worth. Then I help them use their value so they can get to where they want to go in their lives or careers.

It's super important that we know how to use the value that we have. A lot of us know that we have something to offer. But it really doesn't do us any good if we can't actually articulate that to those who matter. Out of this premise, The VALUE method was born.

V.A.L.U.E. is actually an acronym that stands for using your Voice to Advocate so others can Learn and Understand your Excellence. Again, we are all excellent and amazing at something. The key is to leverage that value so that we can achieve our goals. Sometimes, you have to say things *differently* to *different* people. Sometimes you have to go about things in a different way. You have to be creative. At the end of the day, you have all of these tools available to you, but you need to know how to use the tools that you have in your toolbox. And that is exactly what I empower you to do as The VALUE Coach.

I've been passed up for opportunities, jobs, promotions, raises, and I have had people that were less qualified than me, specifically white males, make more money than I have. NEVER AGAIN! I don't want another woman to have to feel the way I felt in those situations. And that is the calling and purpose of this book and what I help hundreds of women everyday do as The VALUE Coach. *Sis, You CAN Negotiate!* This book will deliver ten extremely valuable tips on how to negotiate your next salary or raise. If you are currently seeking a new role within your current company or another desired company, or if you could use a raise in your current one (and who couldn't use a raise), this is the book you've been waiting for. Keep reading. Time to get to work.

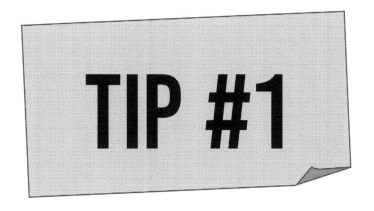

Know Your VALUE!

IT'S IMPOSSIBLE TO GET YOUR value if you don't *know* your value. You can't go to the table trying to negotiate when you don't even know what it is that you have to offer. So before you can do that, make sure you know what your value consists of. This is probably the most important step in the entire process. But this is also the step that a lot of people miss, and have a hard time doing it. Your value is literally everything you bring to the table. So, what is *your* value?

To get started, I want you to think about these questions: In what things, do you excel? What do you do well, superiorly even? What are you passionate about? What do people call you for? How can you help in a way no one else can?

I guarantee you each and every one of you has a friend, a family member or someone who calls you whenever they have a problem with something. And it doesn't necessarily have to be a typical technical skill. Are you really good at cooking? Are you really good at connecting people? Are you good at calming people down when they get angry? These are all valuable skills

3

you could bring to the table at home and at work. You deserve to take the time to designate and specify them.

What I do with my VALUE method is help my clients craft what I call their VALUE Statement. Your VALUE Statement is a brief elevator pitch, but focused on your value. Your VALUE Statement will need to answer these three basic questions: 1. Who are you? 2. How do you add value? 3. Why should someone care?

When you are seeking to uplevel your business or career, people need to know what it is that you can do for them. Do you know how many people I have spoken to about their value, and cannot answer these questions? Some have simply never thought about it, while others do not believe they have value to offer. *What?! Of course you have value to offer!* Here are steps you can take to get started.

First, think of three words that make up your identity. For example, I'm Black, female and Christian. That's me. Realize – and I want to stress this point – you already add a certain level of value just by simply being you. There may be other teachers, other writers, but no one else is YOU. When you are thinking about your identity, I want you to think about words that describe you, but some aspect of your identity is just being uniquely you. Embrace yourself.

Next, brainstorm the things that are not on your resume, things that make you unique or different. I will continue to use myself as an example. I sing in a classical chorale. I exercise through kickboxing and running. It's been amazing! My favorite NFL team is the Dallas Cowboys. (Sidebar: I'm originally from Philadelphia and my family basically disowns me for claiming the Dallas Cowboys as the best NFL team, but I digress.) These interests, activities and hobbies aren't on my resume but they contribute to me being a unique, interesting individual.

Next, brainstorm your strengths. Using myself as an example again, I'm passionate about helping others. It's one of the main reasons that I'm on Earth. I'm a great oral advocate. As an attorney, I've been trained in effective oral and written communication. I'm also a quick learner. I guarantee you, you have something. Take your time on this step until you have identified at least five strengths.

The final step is to combine aspects of what you wrote down into a statement. This may not be the final VALUE Statement that you would use publicly, but it gives you a starting point. As time goes on, you will be better able to identify and articulate your value.

If you find it difficult to start this process of discovering and articulating your value, you are not alone. You have to believe you are valuable *before* you can start getting your value and worth. If you want that higher salary or raise, start by reminding yourself and affirm over and over again "I am valuable!"

REFLECTION QUESTIONS

❖ Who are you?

❖ How do you add value to the world around you?

Bonus Tip: When thinking about your value, emphasize your experience that aligns with the job description of your current or desired job.

Want More? I have a course on How to Craft Your VALUE Statement where I teach you how to refine and deliver your VALUE Statement.

TIP #2

Do Your Research

THIS IS A VERY, VERY important step in the process. Before you can actually start negotiating, you have to spend time researching the company. In some cases, it could be a new salary, company or job. In other cases, you're maybe wanting a raise at your current employer. Regardless, you still need to do research. There are several questions needed to initiate and complete the research process:

What are others in your current position making at the job? That's probably one of the main questions you want to make sure you know, before you go in and negotiate a salary for that position. You need to know what other people are making in that same type of role. And it doesn't even have to be within the same company. Take a look at what other similar organizations pay for that role or something comparable. With the information gathered, you will be able to discern and make an informed decision of the right organization for you. Being armed with options will aid you in advocating for yourself.

You may discover that similar roles may vary in pay and/or value of benefit packages. In all the roles that I have acquired over the years, I have been able to connect with someone discreetly at my desired place of employment to gather some of the information I needed. (This is another reason why networking is so important). Outside of that, there's a lot that you can find out from some digging on the internet.

It's easy to find out government salaries because it's public information. However, positions in the public sector might require a little more digging. Check out sites like *Glassdoor* and *PayScale*. *Law Crossing* is a great resource for lawyers, as well as *LinkedIn* for many white collar positions. Sometimes unfortunately, the information is not going to be available. Sometimes you literally just don't know. And that's where your network and researching similar positions in other companies will help you. Even if you just have an idea of what people in that general position are making, it's better than going into any new situation blindly. There's a lot of free information out there, so don't be afraid to use all of your resources to find out what options are available to you.

You also want to make sure that you know what it actually looks like to work within that organization, exploring company culture and protocol. So that's really helpful when you have somebody that's actually been there before. For my lawyers, what are the billable hour requirements? You must know how many hours you are going to be expected to work there. How many of those hours will be in-office hours and how many can be worked from home? It can look appealing when your current job is paying you for instance, $70,000 and your desired job is paying $90,000. However, if your current job only requires you to bill 1800 hours, and your desired job requires you to bill 2000 hours, that's a noticeable difference, affecting your quality of life. In terms of time, you must ask yourself, is it worth it for you? In your research process, you will have an opportunity to actually secure the answers to these questions.

Assuming that you get your desired position and receive a formidable offer, you must also continue your research of the position and company during the interview process. Your interview does not just involve the company interviewing you, but you are interviewing the company. You are literally doing your due diligence, doing your research to find out if this company or organization that you want to work for is a good fit for your goals, lifestyle, and quality of life. Make sure you ask those pertinent questions so that when you finish the interview process and you do get an offer, then you have that information to make as informed of a decision as possible.

I remember a friend of mine was offered what she thought was her dream job. This new job came with a company car and a beautiful office. So why did she quit after only working there for one month? Well, one thing she realized very quickly was that her compensation didn't match what she thought it would be. The role was advertised as $30 an hour with travel time, but she never asked about the compensation for her travel time and administrative work. She was paid $30 an hour while she was meeting with clients but only received $15 an hour for her travel time and administrative hours. Those hours were more than half her time. She didn't get what she expected and that's because she didn't do her research by asking the proper questions.

Another thing to research is the employee hierarchy of the company. As it relates to other key players of the organization: associate secretaries, supervisors, managers, etc., you just want to make sure your role and the roles of your associates are defined. You need to know where you fit on that ladder. Do you have to supervise other people? Are other people supervising you? What's the support staff ratio to attorneys for my lawyers? Those of you in other positions, will you have support of a secretary or assistant? How do you receive your work assignments? Do you have control over your own workload and calendar? What's the structure when somebody's out? These are key questions that sometimes go unasked in the interview process.

The important thing to remember when conducting your research is to take your time. Some answers will be easier to find than others, but stay encouraged. That new salary or raise will be well worth your time.

REFLECTION QUESTIONS

❖ What is the average salary for your desired job in your location?

❖ Who in your network do you need to connect with to find out more information about a job or company?

Bonus Tip: If searching for a new role, think about how the company organizes their data. If the company is paper only and hasn't adopted an electronic system, you may have a lot more work to do to keep things organized depending on what your job is.

TIP #3

Never Give the
First Number

A LOT OF JOBS WILL ask you upfront, either in the interview process, or sometimes even in the cover letter before you apply during your application: What are your salary requirements? In most cases, I don't recommend pinning yourself down to a specific salary so early in the application process. I have found that companies who ask for salary requirements in a cover letter, especially for smaller organizations, use this as a guide to determine whether or not to interview you. If the company knows they only have $100,000 available in their budget to hire someone and you ask for $150,000, even with the right skills, you probably won't receive an invitation to interview.

Many of you have probably applied for a job using a company's career section of their website that requires you to create an account with an email address and password before you can apply. If you are asked for salary requirements/expectations on an application like that, I recommend leaving the questions blank, at least not on formal applications. There are computer systems that are used to search for certain words in applications and resumes, and accept or reject you based on a preliminary scan. When asked your salary requirements on an application, either leave it blank or if required, input $1. The reason for this is because once you put a specified number out there, you are stuck with and carry that number throughout the entire hiring process.

Many times you are asked your desired range, before you have had an opportunity to think about it fully, many times BEFORE you have even had an interview! What happens if you learn something new during the interview process or realize the job will require a lot more work than advertised; and then you are stuck. If you're applying to many jobs, after tirelessly sending application after application, you might just restlessly be ready to put something in the system and just hit send already. You don't want to make that mistake. You want to put yourself in the most advantageous position to make an educated decision about your career future.

A cover letter requires a slightly different approach, especially for attorney positions. Companies love to ask: "What are your salary requirements?" in a job posting. There is a way to answer without answering, pivoting to: "I want a salary that's comparable to others in my position", or "I desire a salary based on my level of experience." When it is a direct email application submission, if you feel more comfortable giving a number (after having done your research), use a salary range within the industry's average for that title/ position.

Some corporate companies like insurance companies like to put the salary range within the job posting, but I'll tell you 9 times out of 10, when that is done, the company plans on offering you something within that range. In some cases, you may be offered something along the higher range. Either way, the listed range is not the real range, it's simply the range that is advertised. Even so, companies love to say a job is "commensurate with experience." It's been my experience that many times this is a code for "We're gonna pay you whatever we feel like paying you. And if you don't ask for enough, we're not going to give you enough."

I've honestly been in positions where I've been financially swindled, simply because the company has certain predetermined pay structures in place. Essentially because other people before you weren't paid fairly, then they will quote pay ranges to how those people valued their worth. In the past, I worked for a firm where there were two female associates that had been working there for about five or six years. I had a good relationship with them, and I actually knew what they were making. When new male associates came to the firm that were at pretty much the same level, they were making $10,000+ more than what the female associates were making, and to add insult to injury, they were new employees. Why? Because the female associates didn't negotiate when they first came onboard.

When I started the salary negotiation process, I was initially told that with their then current pay structure, that they could only offer what they were offering, while garnering various excuses. Some of these probably sound familiar. Maybe it was because they weren't paying the other people that were more senior than me enough. So giving you a salary more comparable to your desired salary could potentially impact the people that come after you.

This also reminds me to address an important point that is often forgotten. Most companies will give you a standard raise each year based on the salary you have. So if you start at a low salary, you can do everything right from that point on and receive your yearly raises and bonuses, but still be underpaid.

So what do you do when you are in a situation where the structure isn't advantageous to you? Many times because of these excuses, the company will ask you for a number first to begin the negotiation process. In these cases, know that you do not have to give your number first. I understand without zeroing on a single number, understanding that whatever that low number is, that's the number on which they will zero in their focus.

For instance, if your target is $100,000, as I say here, you're not going to say, "Oh, well, my salary range is $90,000 - $110,000, or something like that, because then they're going to give you $90,000, which isn't what you actually want. Even if you start at $100,000, they're just going to say, okay, 100, is what she wants, but try to negotiate you down for whatever that number is. So if you really want $100,000, you need to start at a higher number like $115,000. And then make sure that range is broad enough. I usually say at least extend a range of $10,000, which is too minimum in my opinion. I try to extend that to a range of at least $15,000 or $20,000. This gives you enough room so that you could still push your way up. But whatever that low number is, just know that that's the number that they're going to offer you most of the time, even if that is not the number you actually want. Whatever number you pick they are still going to try to knock you down, so choose wisely.

If you are negotiating a raise, and not a new salary, which is a completely different process, then you should give an exact number. It is important that you come to the table with very specific things. Tell your boss or supervisor what you have been able to accomplish extraordinarily in your current role. Therefore, for the aforementioned accomplishments, that is why you request (insert your desired number) that you want right now. That's how you get there. Otherwise, never provide a number first. In the case of a raise, it is the only exception.

Finally, never disclose your current salary. And as an attorney, I consider this very strongly. Each state's laws are different. But in Connecticut, and many other U.S. states, it is illegal to ask a potential candidate's current or past salary. But what happens too often is that interviewees disclose their salary voluntarily simply because they were thinking out loud during the interview instead of thinking about it prior to the interview. So when an employer says something along the lines of: "Hey Stephanie, can you tell me what salary you're looking for?" If Stephanie hasn't fully thought about it, she is most likely going to say, "Yeah, well, I currently make (this amount), so what I want (that amount)."

This is a natural first response. However, you are doing yourself a disservice if you do not come prepared for the conversation. You can disclose a desired salary range WITHOUT disclosing what you currently make.

In the event that an employer asks what your prior or current salary is during an interview, you're not required to answer.[2] I suggest saying: "Well, my current salary isn't relevant to the position that I'm applying

---

[2] Laws may differ on this issue in each state. This is not legal advice. Please consult a lawyer in your state if you have questions.

for here. However, I'd be happy to discuss my salary requirements at a later time once I have some additional information." Chances are they will probably be a little thrown off, but again, you do not have to answer that question. And if they're forcing you or putting you in a position where you feel forced, that might not be an employer you want to work with.

REFLECTION QUESTIONS

❖ What do you do when a potential employer asks you to provide your salary requirements during the application process?

❖ How can you pivot from answering a question about your current salary during an interview?

Bonus Tip: The general rule is to never give the first number, but as mentioned in this chapter, it cannot always be avoided. The key is to be prepared for the question when it is asked.

TIP #4

Never Negotiate in Writing

THE NEGOTIATION PROCESS CAN MOVE very quickly. In fact, the pace of negotiations can sometimes be used as an advantage (or disadvantage) depending on which side of the table you are sitting at. This is why negotiation should always be done face to face, and never within written modes of communication unless absolutely necessary. So much of negotiation is about understanding who is on the other side and being able to pick up on subtle cues. When you have an actual conversation, you can perceive things like voice inflection, body language, and even eye contact that you otherwise would not.

So when you're talking about negotiating in writing, this includes emails, cover letters, and anything you are required to write out. If somebody writes you an offer in writing, that doesn't mean you have to write them back and respond in writing, at least not if you're going to negotiate. If you're just simply going to accept it, go ahead, but I still don't recommend doing that. You should ALWAYS negotiate. Even if you got everything you wanted in that offer, there is always room for more. And sometimes, they expect you to negotiate.

I remember talking to a friend who told me that she got an offer that was exactly what she was looking for. Sadly, her prior job was severely underpaying her. When she decided to look for new employment, she had a salary in mind and would not accept anything less than that. I'm all for it! Well, she got a job offer by email about $5,000 over the number she wanted and accepted it immediately! No negotiation involved. Sound familiar? She found out later on from Human Resources that there was an additional $10,000 for the position. They expected her to counter after the initial offer, but she didn't. She missed out!

So even if you got an offer with your desired salary, or money isn't your first priority, it doesn't mean it is not worth a conversation to clarify the written offer. When you do respond to the offer, do not do it via email because then all you have done is allowed the potential employer to think about what you wrote without your interjection or input, thereby putting them in a position where they can get input from others and think about it, negating yourself out of the negotiation process. How many times have you gotten an email or a text message from someone and you weren't sure how to respond so you waited until you got input from someone else? This same thing can and will happen if you negotiate in writing so it's best to do it over the phone or in person.

I do realize that our "new normal" we are in can sometimes limit our ability to meet in person. However, even if the negotiation must be done virtually in video form, then persist to do that.

REFLECTION QUESTIONS

❖ When is it okay to negotiate in writing?

❖ What is one thing you will look for in terms of body language or voice inflection during your next negotiation ?

Bonus Tip: Just because it may not be advantageous to negotiate officially in writing, doesn't mean you shouldn't first write down your arguments for negotiation. You can use these notes in preparation for the actual conversation.

TIP #5

Know Your Number And Your BATNA

I KNOW MANY OF YOU are probably scratching your head wondering what a BATNA is. It's important to know your number, which is your target salary or the amount of your desired raise. That number should now be secured in your head. But, you must also know your BATNA. This term is used specifically in negotiation, and it stands for the *Best Alternative to a Negotiated Agreement.* Essentially, your BATNA is the best number or the best outcome (depending on what you're negotiating) should you not receive what you desire in the negotiation process. Another way of thinking about your BATNA is what would you have if you walked away from the negotiations and nothing changed.

It's important to note that the BATNA is not just limited to numbers. Your BATNA is what you have in the event that negotiations fall apart. If you're going through the back and forth of negotiation, and it doesn't seem like you are going to resolve it, what's the best situation that could happen after that? What is going to happen if nothing happens the way that you actually want? These are scenarios and outcomes you need to be aware of. For example, if you are negotiating a raise, your BATNA will probably be that you would keep your current salary without any change.

Knowing your BATNA is important, but I want to point out that it is a good idea to not only think about your "best" alternative to a negotiated agreement, but you also want to think about your "worst" alternative to a negotiated agreement, also known as a WATNA. Using the same example as we did above for negotiating a raise to your salary, the worst alternative may be that you lose your job. Of course no one would want that to happen, but thinking about what you have to lose in the process is important to do. Once you have thought about these alternatives, be sure that you never reveal your true number or your BATNA.

Now it's time to decide on your desired target salary number. When negotiating, avoid using round numbers. For instance, let's say my goal is to be offered $50,000. Right now, I'm making $30,000. If I say that I want to be offered $50,000 or $60,000, then it is very likely the potential employer will come back with $40,000 because that is a round number directly in the middle of $30,000 and $50,000. They are predictable. Avoid this at all costs. Instead, give a different number. If you want $50,000, ask for $67,300. Why that number? Because it challenges the employer to think differently about the situation and breaks their logic. When you give easy and middle round touch points, potential employers will think nine times out of ten in terms of round numbers 5, 10, 15, 20. When you avoid doing that, you'll also avoid revealing what your true desired number is and have more leverage for negotiation.

REFLECTION QUESTIONS

❖ What does BATNA stand for?

❖ What are ways you can calculate your BATNA before your next negotiation ?

Bonus Tip: Make sure you differentiate between your target number and your BATNA. While it is possible they will be the same, most likely they will be different. Write down both of them as you prepare to negotiate.

TIP #6

Use Your Worth to Leverage What You Want

WE HAVE COVERED IN SOME detail knowing the worth and value that you bring to the table. Now it is time to leverage that value to get what you want. This is probably one of the most important steps, but the part that many people neglect.

In order to use your value as leverage for what you want, you need to know exactly what value you bring and what you want. Take time and write down all of the amazing things that you have accomplished and done in the span of your career. Literally take out a piece of paper and write it down. You can type it if you prefer digital lists. Sometimes we forget all of the awesomeness that we are and bring to the table. You might have forgotten about that extra client you secured last month, or the benchmark that you exceeded last year. We forget.

Take time to look at your resume, check your emails, your phone, text messages, etc. to jog your memory. Another thing you can do is talk to others close to you including friends, family members or coworkers. The perspective of others can be very helpful during this process.

In the case of pursuing a new job, take a look at the potential employer's job description. Write out the things that you've done in your current or previous that would make you qualified for the desired role. This will create even more leverage on your part. If the job description for instance, says that research is a required skill in the role, then look back at your resume to find where you have done similar research, making you more of a direct fit for the position. If you are pursuing a sales role, and if your desired employer has a certain type of quota required for the position, whatever it is, make sure that you can *check the boxes* that they have for the role based on past quotas you've met, substantiating your contribution. Be prepared to talk specifically about the experience. You can also include this information on your resume and cover letter.

With the clients in my coaching program, I help them properly communicate these specified assets in all communication modes with the employer, via resume, interview and cover letter. I believe it's super important that you know all of the amazing things that you bring to the table. For those of you seeking promotion within your current companies and want to present or remind your current employer of your metrics, I guarantee you that nine times out of ten, your boss and manager do not keep track of your performance. They don't. They are not paying attention to you that closely. Some positions are the exception if within a smaller environment.

When you're working for larger companies, usually your boss is too busy, and they are preoccupied with all the other stuff they have to do. Now, I'm not saying they don't recognize the overall contribution you bring to the team, but they're not tracking everything. So in these cases, you HAVE to remind them of what you did. When you go to your boss and ask for a raise, without knowing the quantifiable impact you have had on your team and the company as a whole, you can expect to eventually get brushed off. But when you go to ask them for that raise, and you come correct with your stats and receipts if you will, detailing how you consistently met quantifiable goal after quantifiable goal and have exceeded expectations, well then, you now have leveraging power to continue a real conversation.

When gathering your quantifiables, it's important to think about the mission of the desired organization. Acknowledging the organization's overall goal, mission or focus, have you been able to do things, maybe even outside of the work environment that in so many words, have made the company look good? Perhaps you are on the board of another nonprofit or business entity in which your contribution is transferable to your current organization. When you supersede those expectations, make sure that you're bringing it to the attention of your desired company, even if they are not *paying* attention. They may have simply overlooked how amazing you're doing. Advocate for yourself and inform them of your excellence, further cementing why you deserve that additional raise.

Another good method of leveraging your worth is to start by revisiting and reviewing your original job description. It's my guess that most of you are doing way more than what is in your actual job description, especially if you've been with the company for a long time. Many times job descriptions are vague as a disadvantage to the employee.

When you actually get into the everyday duties of the position, you realize you're doing like 10 or 15 different things, many which are not on your job description. Many times after a coworker has left the company for whatever reason, you may find yourself doing their job too. Many times we assume the responsibilities of the abandoned role *temporarily* and temporarily slowly becomes permanently, as the company drags their feet, able to get the work of two jobs done for the price of one employee: *you*. Reacquaint yourself with all you do and have done, reminding the employer of your contribution to leverage the position you want.

REFLECTION QUESTIONS

❖ What are requirements that stand out to you in your current job description?

❖ What are three things you have done in the past 5 years that qualify you for a raise or for the job you are seeking?

TIP #7

Be Creative With Your Options

EARLIER, WE TALKED ABOUT KNOWING *your number*, but sometimes being too inflexible about that number would put you in a problematic situation. That number is just your target, a starting place. If you know you want $100,000 as your salary, great, but there may be some other ways to get that $100,000 value within a diversified employee package. In other words, other factors and aspects of that offer can still get you to where you want to be.

For example, maybe you could negotiate remote working days. You could also potentially leverage additional vacation or PTO days. However, don't fool yourself. If you are so "busy" and you never use or get approved to use those vacation days, then you lose that value and are depreciating your own package. To safeguard against this, research the company culture and policy regarding using vacation days. Does the company pay for unused vacation days? Do any of your vacation days from the prior year rollover to the following year? If so, how many days?

When I left one of my insurance company employers, I received close to a $4,000 payday, not as a severance but because I was working my ass off, and I did not take many days off. Because the company paid for unused vacation time, I got a nice little paycheck when I left. At the end of the day, your desired job may not be your *forever* job, depending on your career goals and opportunities for upward mobility. Discover and self -reflect on the job you want to have, your "why" for being in your current position, and what career progression would be needed for you to reach your ultimate career goals.

In COVID and post-COVID times, more companies are offering full or partial work from home opportunities than ever before. If you have kids at home, and need that flexibility, negotiate it in, even if you are able to work two or three days from home during the week.

In other cases, you can leverage your position title, because title can matter quite a bit in some industries. And let me say this so there is no confusion. As I have stated before, your value is NOT tied to a title. But, in some cases a title may matter more. For example, if you have your eye on changing companies in the future and know that a "Director" gets paid more than a "Manager" it may be worth advocating for the title that can lead to upward mobility faster. There is a huge difference between a manager, supervisor or senior, director, etc., especially if the company doesn't care about the actual title of the position as long as the job duties are fulfilled.

The point I am making here is that you have the power to advocate for whatever it is you want! Don't feel limited by just negotiating your salary if other aspects of the job are more important to you.

REFLECTION QUESTIONS

❖ What is something you can advocate for in your next job that is not directly tied to the salary or financial compensation?

❖ Why is this something that is important for you to advocate for?

Bonus Tip: If you are in a sales type of role and are paid on commission, don't forget about negotiating a higher base compensation rate or a higher percentage in commission sales.

TIP #8

Negotiate With
The Right Person

I CAN'T TELL YOU HOW difficult it is to try to negotiate with somebody who actually doesn't have the authority to negotiate your package. Without that authority, you're almost wasting your time. If you're not talking to the person that actually makes the decision at the end of the day, then you are relying on the person that you're talking to relay your message. And they don't have any reason to advocate for you. Most times, they don't even know you and aren't on your team. They're going to summarize what you've said. Sometimes they even lie about what you've said or about the fact that they said your petition was rejected when they never actually presented your petition. I've been in situations where I've made my petition to a go-between and was told my requests were denied, only to fact-check later and discover they never presented my requests at all, and there was more room to negotiate my desires than they had let on.

Realize *you* and only *you* have your best interest at heart. Your company has its best interest at heart as well. Anytime that you can get in front of the actual decision maker, do it. But in order to do so, you must know who's in what position. This goes back to doing your research. Because you need to know who's in what position. Doing your research could result in you speaking directly with the head of HR, as opposed to the recruiter, who at the end of the day, is essentially a middleman and isn't really making the decisions. The company hires that person to be the middleman to have those conversations with you that the higher-up doesn't want to have.

With positions that require advocating and negotiating within the job duties, for example for those duties of an attorney, being acclimated to negotiation is probably expected by the employer. In many cases, my main job role was to negotiate. If I failed to do so in the hiring process, and didn't negotiate my salary, what would that say about my capability to handle the negotiating aspects of my job? Many firms, especially law firms will leave room negotiation on purpose. They *want* and are *expecting* you to negotiate. But what you don't ask for, you don't get.

Once you have asked for what you want, keep in mind that a hiring representative goes back to their hiring committee and says something like: "Hey Amanda, applied for this new sales associate position. This is what she asked for her salary… we want approval, yes or no." They're usually not a lot of back and forth behind closed doors. So if at all possible, speak to the person at the top.

In some cases, you can negotiate PTO after being hired by the company, more so doing your annual review. Review how PTO is accrued and how it can be altered to meet your desires. But remember, unless this option is engrafted in your contract, your company is not obligated to provide more PTO for you. That is why negotiating on the front end is crucial.

When negotiating things like additional PTO or a title change, try to follow up in writing, confirming the conversation and date and with whom you spoke. Yes, verbal agreements are valid but this ensures that the firm is held accountable.

REFLECTION QUESTIONS

❖ Who is the person typically responsible for making the final decisions on salary and compensation at your current or future organization?

❖ If you cannot speak to the decision-maker directly, what are some strategies you can do to help ensure your position is adequately conveyed on your behalf?

Bonus Tip: If you are unsure of who the best person is to negotiate with, try looking for the organizational chart for the company. This will detail who is in what role/position and their rank/authority in the company.

TIP #9

Don't Leave Money on the Table

AFTER THE BACK AND FORTH of negotiations, some processes move quickly while some move a little slower, but at some point, you are going to have to simply say yes or no. If they are giving you an offer, it sounds good to you, you've hit your numbers and you're thinking about it and just kind of deciding, it's fine. If you need a little bit of time to think, that's okay. But after a while, it will be time to make a decision. So you really can only do one of three things. You either take the offer, leave the offer or counter. That's it.

Again, it's okay to think about things. But when there's been a long back and forth process, you don't want to leave the employer too much time to reconsider. I'm not saying don't think about the offer because sometimes these processes can take a couple weeks. I've had clients who have told me that their negotiation processes had taken a couple months. In those types of cases, I don't even know if you would want to work for those types of companies. It shouldn't be *that* hard.

You've said what you want. They're either going to give it or not.

Still, in the situations that have worked out in my favor, it's usually been pretty quick. They present the offer. You review it. You've already done your due diligence, have researched and mapped it all out; You counter saying, *Listen, this is what I need. This is option one, if you can't do that, okay, here's option two.*

However, do not shoot yourself in the foot in the presentation of your *options.* First, put your best offer out there and then wait to see what they say. Only after that, come back and say, *Okay, figure it out. Here's option two,* but you want to make sure that you are not leaving money on the table.

Here is a quick lesson in contract law for my non-lawyers. An offer can be rejected at any time before it is accepted, so it is important to accept the offer if that is what you plan to do. BUT it's important to note that once you start to negotiate, you are rejecting the offer as it stands and put the power back in the hands of your soon to be employer, and they can use that power to say no! That's called a counteroffer. It's rare, but it does happen. One of my friends from law school had a firm reject her counteroffer and hired someone else, so keep this in mind during your negotiation process.

REFLECTION QUESTIONS

❖ What is it called when you have received an offer and responded with additional terms to negotiate?

❖ Why is it important to accept an offer if you are satisfied and don't have additional terms to negotiate?

Bonus Tip: You can also attempt to accept certain aspects of the offer and leave other aspects on the table, even after your start date including vacation time, but I would only use this strategy in limited circumstances.

TIP #10

Don't Be Afraid
to Walk Away!

WALKING AWAY IS ONE OF those things that sometimes I think we forget that we have the power to do. But that's it. Don't be afraid to walk away. You're putting yourself out there, so I know it might not be something that you want to do after time has been invested in the negotiation process. But sometimes that may be the best thing to do. Knowing your value means saying no when you aren't getting it. If you have spent the time understanding your value, worth, your *number*, and they're still saying no, then it may just be a no. That means this isn't the right fit, firm or position for you.

It's been said that "*no*" just stands for the *next opportunity*. Keep it moving. You cannot be afraid to walk away. Knowing your value and your worth starts with confidence. No one else can tell you how great and awesome you are better than you can. Sometimes others will acknowledge your greatness, sometimes on a rare occasion, your manager might come into your office and say, "You know what Angelica? You've been doing such a great job this year. I want to give you a raise and a promotion." And you don't even see it coming. Yes, that *could* happen. But it's very rare. Sis, you have to be willing to walk away if the company or organization isn't seeing your worth and value.

When we're talking about asking for a raise, you want to know where you stand at the end of the conversation as well. Even if it doesn't go the way that you desire, at least you initiated the conversation. And that's okay. It may be a no for now, but in the back of your mind, your wheels start to turn. *Maybe I don't need to stay here anymore. What am I doing next? Let me start interviewing. Let me start seeing what else is out there.* Even if you don't walk away with what you requested, you now have more clarity on my options.

Personally, in every single job I've had, regardless of how content I was in my role or company, I was always interviewing, keeping my options open. In my case, I actually ended up working for myself, because at the end of the day, that's what God purposed me to do anyway. Whether you are better suited for entrepreneurial ventures, a corporate position or potentially a combination of the two, you have to remain in a state if readiness. If you stay ready, you don't have to get ready. So scope out opportunities, see what's going on out there and continue to put yourself out there because where you are may not be your final destination. And you can't wait for your current employer to recognize your worth. It's super important to note when your time has expired and it's time to move on.

But what we *don't* want to do is say, "Well, you know what, screw y'all. I quit." No sis, don't do that. You may *want* to do that. But don't. You want to make sure you keep all relationships as intact as possible, never burning bridges when possible, further preserving your professional reputation. Walk away respectfully from all negotiating conversations, even if they don't end in your favor. This leaves the door open to revisit again if necessary.

Sometimes the desired employer may not have the ability to give what you request at that particular time. Some may say, *We, at your annual review in six months,* or *When we secure this merger in three months…,* or *After we get over this hump in six months- then we can re-talk.* Hold them to that. I would even recommend following up with a written communication saying something along the lines of: *I appreciated our conversation. Thank you for all of the above, [insert the positive takeaways from the conversation]. Let's revisit this at the later date that we discussed."*

Let's say the employer says, *Oh, we can't give you a raise right now. However, if you hit [X, Y, Z] number of sales within the next six months, or if you build this many hours in [this time period], then you'll be eligible.* Get that in writing because now you have something to hold them to. I actually had an employer *try* to tell me I wasn't eligible for a raise or bonus within my role. And I pointed them right back to my offer letter, and they had to honor it. I held them to what they said. Maybe they meant to say something else, but I read my offer *very* carefully and you should too.

These things are geared for guaranteed success. One of my clients literally worked with me for a 30-minute strategy session where we deep dived into these tips, and she was able to negotiate $15,000 above her last offer, plus a title change. These tips matter! And what you want matters, sis. It is crucial as women that we have to understand our value and put ourselves out there. No one else is going to do it for you. Others won't recognize your worth, goodness, and pure amazingness that you bring to the table. All that you are doing and contributing. But we know and we can't be afraid to ask for what we are worth.

I believe it was Shirley Chisholm who said: "If they don't give you a seat at the table, bring a folding chair." That's a great quote. And nothing against Shirley Chisholm. She's an amazing woman, and even ran for president. But for me, I'm of the mindset that if you don't want me at your table, that's okay because I can find another or better yet build my own. So say "I don't need a seat at your table. And I'm not bringing a folding chair. I'll build my own table and sit on a throne!" Better yet, I'm going to build a throne covered with gold and rubies. Because I'm a high value woman and we as high value women deserve the excellence that we are!

FINAL THOUGHTS

Thank you for reading this book. I initially provided these 10 tips in a workshop I did in 2021. Although I am only publishing it in 2023 along with many other titles I've been working on, I hope you find the 10 tips helpful and useful to you.

If you want to learn more about the work I do and see what I have going on, check out my website at aignegoldsby.com.

And if no one has told you this today, remember that you are VALUABLE!

ABOUT THE AUTHOR

AIGNÉ GOLDSBY is an attorney, speaker, diversity consultant, and career coach helping future and current lawyers successfully navigate the attorney journey. She is also passionate about diversity and impacting the personal and professional lives of others. Attorney Goldsby received her J.D. from the University of

Connecticut School of Law and her B.A. from Bryn Mawr College.

Attorney Goldsby in the Founder of Goldsby Law, PLLC and Black Esquire LLC. Attorney Goldsby's coaching method focuses on VALUE. VALUE stands for using your VOICE to ADVOCATE so others can LEARN and UNDERSTAND your EXCELLENCE. Attorney Goldsby enjoys using her voice to speak to audiences worldwide for lasting impact and change. You can learn more about Aigné Goldsby on her website at aignegoldsby.com.

Printed in the United States
by Baker & Taylor Publisher Services